My Sibling Story:

A Companion Workbook to *Billy's Sister*

by Jessica Leving

A Project of The Center for Siblings of People with Disabilities

My Sibling Story:
A Companion Workbook to "Billy's Sister"

All Rights Reserved.
Copyright © 2020 Jessica Leving and The Center for Siblings of People with Disabilities

The opinions expressed in this manuscript are solely the opinions of the author. The author has represented and warranted full ownership and/or legal rights to publish all of the materials in this book.

This book may not be reproduced, transmitted or stored in whole or in part without the express written consent of the author.

Published by The Center for Siblings of People with Disabilities
www.siblingcenter.org

PRINTED IN THE UNITED STATES OF AMERICA

What's the title of YOUR story?

_____

www.siblingcenter.org

What's your name? _____

What's your sibling's name? _____

Me:	My sibling(s):

What's the name of your sibling's disability?

_____

How does it affect them?
Write or draw an example below.

www.siblingcenter.org

Everyone has things they're good at, and things that are harder.

What are some things you're good at?

I'M GOOD AT:

```
┌─────────────────────────────────────────┐
│                                         │
│                                         │
│                                         │
│                                         │
└─────────────────────────────────────────┘
```

What are some things that are harder?

HARD FOR ME:

```
┌─────────────────────────────────────────┐
│                                         │
│                                         │
│                                         │
└─────────────────────────────────────────┘
```

What is your sibling good at?

MY SIBLING IS GOOD AT:

```
┌─────────────────────────────────────────────────┐
│                                                 │
│                                                 │
│                                                 │
│                                                 │
└─────────────────────────────────────────────────┘
```

What are some things that are harder?

HARD FOR MY SIBLING:

```
┌─────────────────────────────────────────────────┐
│                                                 │
│                                                 │
│                                                 │
│                                                 │
└─────────────────────────────────────────────────┘
```

www.siblingcenter.org

What are some things you and your sibling like to do together?

Circle all the activities below that you enjoy!

- **Reading**
- **Watching TV**
- **Playing with LEGOS**
- **Telling ghost stories**
- **Playing with dolls**
- **Playing video games**

- **Playing pretend**
- **Arts and crafts**
- **Cooking**
- **Swimming**
- **Sports**
- **Playing with pets**

Did we miss one?
Write or draw it here!

www.siblingcenter.org

What are some of your favorite foods? What are some of your sib's favorite foods?

Do you have any of the SAME favorite foods?

www.siblingcenter.org

Most siblings don't get along 100% perfectly ALL the time. Are there ever times when your brother or sister annoys you?

Write or draw an example below!

What does your face look like when you're ANNOYED?

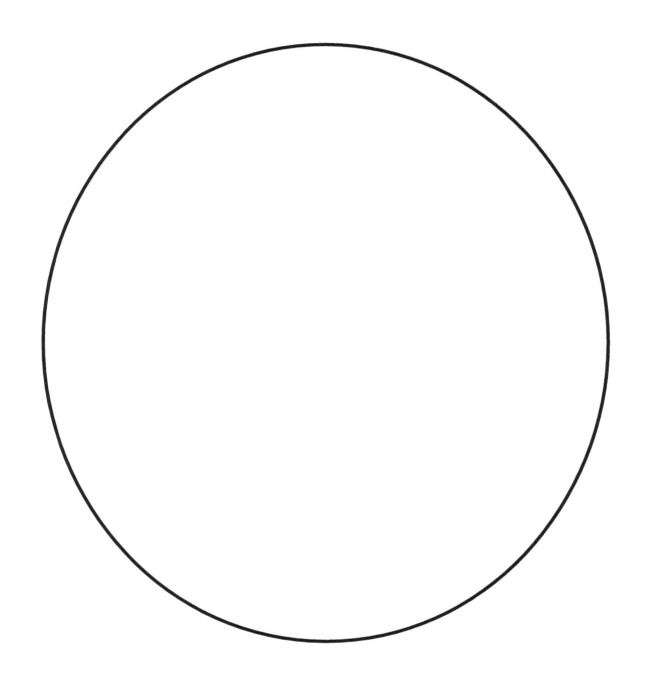

www.siblingcenter.org

What about when you're ANGRY?

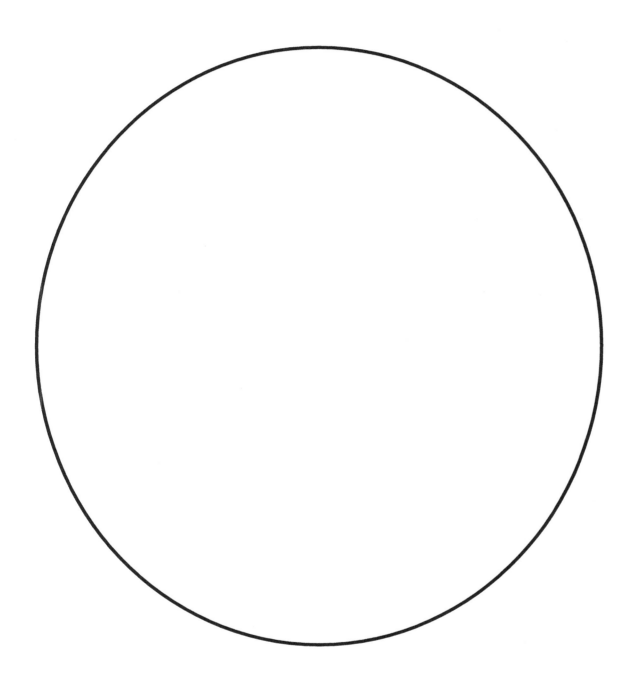

www.siblingcenter.org

Maybe you act like a scary monster!

www.siblingcenter.org

Or maybe you keep it all stuffed inside, like a volcano rumbling secretly beneath a mountain.

www.siblingcenter.org

Or maybe you SCREAM, like Jessica does in the book!

www.siblingcenter.org

Here are some of the things Jessica likes to do when she feels annoyed or angry.

Draw an "X" next to the ones you think might be a good idea to try!

_____ Take a deep breath

_____ Write in my journal

_____ Draw a picture of my feelings

_____ Cook, play sports, or do another fun activity

_____ Call a friend on the phone

_____ Squeeze a stress ball

_____ Hug my dog or cat (or other pet)

_____ Talk to a trusted grown-up about how I'm feeling

www.siblingcenter.org

If you picked "Talk to a trusted grown-up about how I'm feeling", who would be a few grown-ups you could talk to? Maybe a parent, grandparent, or teacher?

Draw them below—and don't forget to write their names!

Sometimes we can also feel embarrassed when our brothers or sisters do things in public or in front of our friends that we wish they wouldn't.

Have you ever felt embarrassed?
What did it feel like?

Write or draw about it below.

Do you ever feel worried that you don't know how to explain your brother or sister's disability to a friend?

Ask a parent or other grown-up to help you come up with one or two sentences, and write it below.

Now you'll have it here next time you need it!

_____

_____

_____

_____

_____

_____

_____

www.siblingcenter.org

Speaking of how to explain stuff... do you ever feel like you have to explain what your sibling is saying, even to your own parents?

Like you guys are speaking your own secret sibling language?

www.siblingcenter.org

What's your favorite thing about your sibling? Write or draw below.

www.siblingcenter.org

What's your favorite thing about YOURSELF? Write or draw below.

Jessica says in the book that writing down her thoughts in a journal is part of how she decided to become a writer.

Can you link the following activities to the jobs they match?

Writing in a journal	**Athlete**
Drawing pictures	**Veterinarian**
Cooking	**Singer**
Playing sports	**Artist**
Reading	**Actor**
Taking care of pets	**Writer**
Playing make-believe	**Chef**
Singing	**Librarian**

www.siblingcenter.org

What do you want to be when YOU grow up?

Write or draw below.

On page 27 of *Billy's Sister,* Jessica drew a family photo of all the people who live in her house.

What would YOUR family photo look like?

www.siblingcenter.org

What kind of place do you want to live when you grow up? Would you like to have an apartment in the city, or a house in the county?

Who do you think might live with you when you grow up? Can you draw them in your pretend future house or apartment below?

What kind of home do you think your sibling would want to have when they grow up? Who do you think might live with them?

How do you feel when you think about the future? Circle as many as you want!

www.siblingcenter.org

How are you feeling RIGHT NOW?

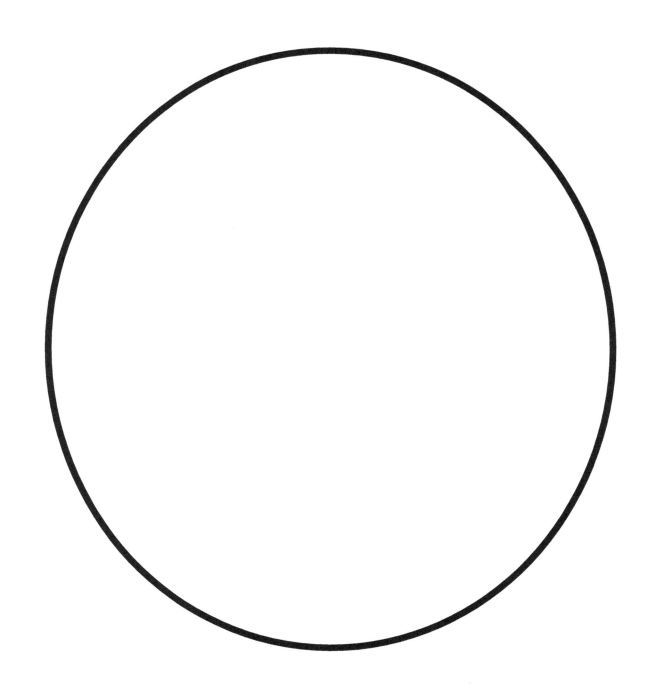

www.siblingcenter.org

Great job—you finished the whole activity book!

Now choose your favorite page, and share it with one of your trusted grown-ups!

www.siblingcenter.org

Made in the USA
Coppell, TX
07 February 2021